सीतायनम्

The Four Lettered Mantra of Rama
for
Rama Jayam - Likhita Japam Mala

Journal for Writing the 4-Lettered Rama Mantra

चतुरक्षर राम मंत्र

व

राम जयम - लिखित जपम

राम-नाम लेखन माला

Belongs to _____

Published by: **Rama-Nama Journals**
(an Imprint of e1i1 Corporation)

Title: **The Four Lettered Mantra of Rama, for Rama Jayam - Likhita Japam Mala**
Sub-Title: **Journal for Writing the 4-Lettered Rama Mantra**

Author: **Sushma**

Copyright Notice: **Copyright © e1i1 Corporation © Sushma**
All rights reserved. No part of this publication may be reproduced, distributed, or transmitted in any form or by any means, including photocopying, recording, or other electronic or mechanical methods.

<u>Identifiers</u>
ISBN: **978-1-945739-34-7** (Paperback)

—o—

www.**e1i1**.com -- www.**OnlyRama**.com
email: **e1i1**books**e1i1**@gmail.com

Our books can be bought online, or at Amazon, or any bookstore. If a book is not available at your neighborhood bookstore they will be happy to order it for you. (Certain Hardcover Editions may not be immediately available—we apologize)

Some of our Current/Forthcoming Books are listed below. Please note that this is a partial list and that we are continually adding new books. Please visit www.**e1i1**.com / www.**onlyRama**.com for current offerings.

- **Tulsi Ramayana—The Hindu Bible:** Ramcharitmanas with English Translation & Transliteration
- **Tulsi-Ramayana Rama-Nama Mala (multiple volumes):** Legacy Journals for Writing the Rama Name alongside Tulsidas Ramcharitmanas—contains English Translation & Transliteration, Inspirational Quotes of Hindu saints, and space for you to jot down your spiritual sentiments on a daily basis. Once embellished with your Rama-Namas, these books become priceless treasures which you can present to your loved ones—a true gift of love, labor, caring, wishing, and above all—Devotion.
- **Ramcharitmanas:** Ramayana of Tulsidas with Transliteration (in English)
- **Ramayana, Large:** Tulsi Ramcharitmanas, Hindi only Edition, Large Font and Paper size
- **Ramayana, Medium:** Tulsi Ramcharitmanas, Hindi only Edition, Medium Font and Paper size
- **Ramayana, Small:** Tulsi Ramcharitmanas, Hindi only Edition, Small Font and Paper size
- **Sundarakanda:** The Fifth-Ascent of Tulsi Ramayana
- **RAMA GOD:** In the Beginning - Upanishad Vidya (Know Thyself)
- **Purling Shadows:** And A Dream Called Life - Upanishad Vidya (Know Thyself)
- **Fiery Circle:** Upanishad Vidya (Know Thyself)
- **Rama Hymns:** Hanumān-Chalisa, Rama-Raksha-Stotra, Bhushumdi-Ramayana, Nama-Ramayanam, Rama-Shata-Nama-Stotra, etc. with Transliteration & English Translation
- **Rama Jayam - Likhita Japam Mala alongside Sacred Hindu Texts (several):** Journals for Writing the Rama Name 100,000 Times alongside various Hindu Texts, with English Translation & Transliteration. Embellish these Books with your Rama-Namas and they become transformed into priceless treasures which you can later gift to your loved ones.
- **Rama Jayam - Likhita Japam Mala alongside Rama-Mantras (several):** Journals for Writing the Rama Name alongside the Rama-Mantras from one lettered to thirty-two & others. Embellish these with your Rama-Namas and they become transformed into priceless treasures.
- **Legacy Books - Endowment of Devotion (multiple volumes)** hers. Legacy Journals for Writing the Rama Name alongside Sacred Hindu Texts

-- On our website may be found links to renditions of Rama Hymns –
-- Rama Mantras/Hymns/Pictures are also available printed on Quality Shirts from Amazon. See our website for details –

rāma-nāma mahimā

As per *Hindu-Darshan* (philosophy), there is just a one-Consciousness which pervades the Universe, with nothing else besides; and the very nature of that consciousness is Bliss. And yet, though our essential nature is rooted in Bliss, still most of us live in misery. Why? Well, according to Tulsīdās, a gemstone is counted a stone and is not valued until it becomes identified by the name. In the same way, the one immortal, true, sentient, complete, and blissful all-pervading Brahmm persists in bondage and suffering (as the visible woeful creation), until becoming revealed into a definite name—energized by the Name 'Rāma'.

Rāma is Bliss. राम, the Rāma-Nāma—Name of Rāma, is the key to that Bliss.

The potency of Rāma-Nāma is unsurpassed in all the four Yugas; the Vedas and other scriptures sing of its glories; and the saints swear by it—especially so in the present Age. In the Kali-Yuga, the chanting of Rāma-Nāma राम is regarded as most-effective and most-supreme—being that in such iniquitous Times, there is no other easy means of salvation.

The present Kali-Yuga, the Iron-Age, is rightly described as vile and sinful. It is awash with the six Gunas of Māyā: *Kāma* (Lust), *Krodha* (Anger), *Lobha* (Greed), *Moha* (Infatuation), *Mada* (Pride) & *Mātsarya* (Envy)—and here we find our minds sinking in worldliness despite our best intentions. Seemingly none can remain unsullied from the taints of Kali—this appears to be the fait-accompli of the Kali-Yuga—a very sad state indeed. But despair not, for when it comes to attaining salvation, many consider this Kali-Yuga to be the Golden-Age. Yes, Kali-Yuga has this one great blessing: through a very simple expediency—simply by a complete surrender to the Holy Name Rāma—one is able to attain to that very high divine state, that very supreme seat, which sages scarcely attained to even after practicing great penances and sacrifices in former Ages.

In the Sata-Yuga, contemplation; in the Tretā, sacrifice; and in the Dwāpar-Yuga worship—these were the appointed propitiations; but in this vile and impure Kali-Yuga—where the soul of man is alike a hapless fish floating in the ocean of sin—in such dreadful times, the Nāma is the only tree of eternal life; and by meditating upon it all the vile commotions become stilled. In these Times neither good deeds, nor piety, nor spiritual wisdom is of any avail—but only the Name of Rāma. The Rāma-Nāma is, as it were, the wisdom and might of Hanumān that exposes and destroys the Kālnemī-like wiles of the wicked world.

Sing the praises of the Lord and remain engaged in *Nāma-Smarana*—is the advice given to us by our saints; the Japa of Rāma-Nāma is the supreme path to salvation—assure our Scriptures; there is no Dharma higher than Nāma-Dharma in this Age—aver the wise. The chanting of Rāma-Nāma is The-One-Supreme-Path to escape the clutches of Kali-Yuga—declares Rāmacharitmānas; in fact it is the one and only Dharma which is easy and feasible given the vicious nature of the present Times.

Well do our scriptures repeatedly assert: In this Kali-Yuga, there is no other means, no other means, no other means of salvation—other than chanting the holy name Rāma, chanting the holy name Rāma, chanting the holy name Rāma.

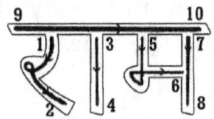

To write राम *in Sanskrit, trace the contours 1-2 (which is the sound of r in 'run'), 3-4 (the sound **a** in '**a**rk'), 5-6 & 7-8 (the sound **m** in '**m**ust') and lastly make the line 9-10.*

Talking of the Rāma-Nāma, Tulsīdās says: रा , म are the two most gracious syllables, the eyes as it were of the soul, the miracle charms which satisfy one's every wish, a gain for this world and felicity in the next. These are nectar-like syllables which stand together united, and are most delightful to utter and hear, and easy to remember. Love naturally gets stirred up as we speak these two mystic syllables: syllables which abide together as inseparably as Rāma and Lakshman, or like the duo Nārayana & Nara; syllables which are as intimately connected as the Universal-Soul and the individual-soul; syllables that are preservers of the world and redeemers of the elect; syllables that shine resplendent like two bright jewels on the ears of Bhakti—Beauteous Devotion; syllables that are pure and beneficent as the Sun and the Moon; syllables that are like sweetness and contentment—the inseparable attributes of ambrosia; syllables that are as inseparable as the hovering bee of devout-souls to the lotus of the Supreme-Soul.

Yogis—who are full of dispassion and detached from the world—are able to keep awake in the daylight of wisdom repeating these two syllables of the Name of Rāma, and thus enjoy the incomparable felicity of Brahmm-Rāma—who is incomparable, unspeakable, unmixed with sorrow and void of name and form. *Gyanis*—those who aspire for knowledge—are able to understand all the mysteries by repeating the Name Rāma. *Sadhaks* (Strivers), who repeat the Name Rāma, absorbed in contemplation, become workers of miracles and acquire great mystic powers. They, who repeat it when burdened with affliction, are freed from their troubles and become blissful and content.

There are four kinds of devotees, and all the four are virtuous, sinless, and noble, and all the four—clever as they are—rely upon the Rāma Name राम. Even those—who are free from all desires and remain ever absorbed in the joy of devotion to Shrī Rāma—throw their heart as fish into the nectarine lake of affection for the Name Rāma.

In all the four ages; in all times, past, present, or future; in the three spheres of earth, heaven and hell—any creature that repeats the name Rāma becomes blessed. The name of Rāma is like the tree of paradise, the centre of all that is good in the world; and whoever meditates upon it verily becomes transformed—from the vile to holy.

As Narasingh was manifested to destroy Hiranyā-kashyap, the enemy of heaven—in order to protect Prahlād—so is राम, the Name of Rāma, for the destruction of the wicked and the protection of the pious.

The chanting of Rāma-Nāma is a direct way to liberation. By repeating this name—whether in joy or in sadness, in activity or in repose—bliss is diffused all around. According to the Vedas, just as the sun dispels the darkness, the chanting of Rāma-Nāma dispels all the evils and obstacles of life. The Rāma Nāma cures agony and showers the blessings of God; all righteous wishes get fulfilled; jealousy and pride disappear; life becomes imbued with satisfaction and peace; all of life's needs fall in place automatically—just like a miracle of nature guiding nature's forces. You may not always get what you want in the exact same form, but the Rāma-Nāma will purify things and bring to you the same needed happiness and bliss in a much more refined and lasting way. Life truly becomes filled with tranquility. With the Rāma-Nāma, an immense sense of spiritual wellbeing is experienced apart from a gain of material happiness.

Rāma-Japa—the constant repetition of the Supreme-Mantra 'Rāma'—is usually done mentally, or on a rosary; but there is one extremely efficacious method of this Japa: the Likhita-*Japa*, or the Written-Chant. The practice of writing the Rāma Mantra over and over on paper is called the Likhita-Japa.

This written form of Japa is a lasting record of your chant, remaining ever imbued with those holy vibrations, for all times, for the benefit of you and the future generations. In India, as you may know, devotees of God have been chanting the name 'Rāma' राम and writing the Name 'Rāma' राम—pages upon pages of it, running into billions and billions, for ages. Hindu children are taught to write the राम Rāma-Nāma from their childhood.

The Likhita Rāma-Nāma Japa is a powerful and transformative tool. As you write the Rāma-Nāma, all the senses become engaged in the service of the Lord-God, and you find yourself simultaneously chanting and hearing and contemplating on the Lord—everything comes together naturally. This method clears away your thoughts and helps concentrate the entirety of your soul upon the Divine.

Any Japa is beneficial but somehow writing the Rāma-Nāma राम on paper brings up a great singularity of focus within the mind—and the peace of heart which ensues is something which is not so easily achieved with other forms of Japa. The written form of Rāma-Japa is somehow able to engage those parts of our body-mind continuum which other methods can not—and our meditative stance is able to gain much deeper levels thereby.

Although the Rāma-Mantra is the gateway to higher consciousness and spiritual upliftment, but even at such junctures—when you find yourself in odd situations, where all the paths seem blocked—then just walking away from everything and simply writing the Rāma Nāma, will give you a much needed clarity of thought—and a divine inspiration that will show a way out.

The Rāma Nāma is very transformative: with it you gain a balanced progress in your outside world and the inner. Sant Tulsīdās says in Rāmacharitmānas: Place the Rāma-Nāma Jewel at the threshold, and there will be light both inside and out; i.e. a constant chant of the Rāma-Nāma from the mouth—the doorway to the body—will bring you external materialistic wellbeing, and also an inner spiritual wellness—both. Incredibly, with the Rāma-Nāma, you get to have the best of both the worlds.

There is something special that happens when you write the राम Rāma-Nāma. Peace and tranquility surrounds you as you write the Supreme-Mantra राम. The Rāma-Mantra imparts to you divine strength and great tolerance to withstand the vicissitudes of life. Bright unclouded wisdom illumines your mind. You find yourself in complete surrender to your inner Being. The resonance of God resonates throughout your mind-body continuity. You feel a flux of divine energy resonating within. You get great power and peace in your everyday life. The Japa of Rāma Mantra protects our inner world as well as the outside.

These journals are for performing the written-Japa of the Rāma-Mantras. Please note that at certain places in the Rāma-Rahasya Upanishad, it is advised to do a certain number of Chants following a prescribed method when trying to pursue a special objective—and you are welcome to follow that regimen separately if you so desire; however the focus of this journal is very simple: a simple introduction to the Mantra, and doing a Written-Japa of that Mantra to gain the grace of Lord Shrī Rāma. Rāma is the most gracious forms of the Lord-God, and He gets pleased through the simplest of means.

This particular edition is for writing the Four-Lettered Rāma-Mantra. A brief introduction of the Mantra is given and it is repeated on every page. A larger Mantra outlines is also printed on each page in case you wish to create a pattern as you write. If you fill this with the Rāma-Mantras using color/size/slant that is different from the outside—then it will also make a large Mantra stand out in the waves of surrounding Rāma-Mantras. Devotees usually make such interesting patterns in their Likhita Japa. Most Devotees will use red ink for writing; some will use different colors to create designs; some will have a special set of pens kept purely for the Likhita in the belief that such implements—that are habitually used for holy tasks—build up energy and holy resonance of their own. There are no hard rules; do what feels natural to you. Also, please feel free to choose any notebook or paper to write upon, not necessarily this Journal.

Please note: if writing these Mantras is too whelming for you, or if you feel hesitant in performing the Japa of Vedic Mantras that should be imparted through formal traditional means, then you can just embellish these pages with simply राम—the Most Supreme Mantra in existence, so sweet and nectar like, and so simple to chant, mutter, write. The 2-Lettered Mantra राम is all-inclusive, all-embracing, universal in scope, with everyone entitled to repeat it without restrictions; especially the *Manasika-Japa*—the silent repetition of राम within the mind—can be performed 24x7, in all situations.

Write the Rāma-Mantra with reverence, every day, preferably at a set time, or as and when possible, in small measures, or copiously—howsoever your situation permits. There are no hard rules, do what feels good to your Soul.

The important thing is to engage in the *Likhita-Japa*—which will lead you on the path to the *Manasika-Japa;* and with time and practice, the Rāma-Nāma राम will flow with your every breath, even while asleep.

When completed, you could keep the Likhita-Japas in your Worship-Room, preserve them as treasures to pass on to future generations, donate them to such Rāma Temples that preserve them, or gift them to your loved ones—who will thereby inculcate crucial values from you and learn the importance of the Rāma-Nāma, and get inspired with Hindu Values, especially so the younger ones.

While writing, focus your mind on the Rāma-Mantra, and chant it within, and hear it in the mind. Imagine Sītā-Rāma showering you with their bliss. Try to stay free of distractions, and with time you will find that your mind will take a natural meditative stance while engaged in the written Rāma-Nāma Japa.

Once embellished with your Rāma-Nāmas, these Journals will become priceless treasures which you can present to your loved ones—an unparalleled gift of love, labor, caring, wishing, and above all—Devotion. We wish you a very blissful Rāma-Nāma Japam.

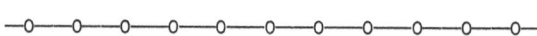

Our following Journals:
Tulsi-Ramayana Rama-Nama Mala (in multiple volumes): Legacy Journals for Writing the Rama Name alongside Full Tulsi Ramayana, are legacy Journals in which you can write down your spiritual sentiments, and the Rāma-Nāma, alongside the printed Tulsi Rāmayana. These Journal-Books contain the original text, transliteration, translation, and space for you to jot down your thoughts and write the Rāma-Nāma. Pages also have inspirational words of Hindu Saint to help guide aspirants on their spiritual journey. You can embellish the entire Tulsi Rāmayana with your Rāma-Nāmas and gift them to your loved ones—a truly unique gift of love, care, labor, and devotion.

Our following Journals:
Rama Jayam - Likhita Japam Mala alongside Sacred Hindu Texts (several)
are Journals for performing the 100,000 Rama-Nama Likhita Japa alongside Sacred Hindu Texts like:
Hanumān Chalisa, Nama Ramayanam, Rama-Ashtottara-Shata-Nama-Valih, Rama-Ashtottara-Shata-Nama-Stotra, Rama Raksha Stotra, Ramashtakam... *(and more on the way)*

the four-lettered mantra of śrī-rāma

Once, the enlightened *Rishis*: Mudgala, Shandilya, Paingala, Bikshu etc.—all distinguished seers who were skilled in philosophy and science, prodigious masters of penance & austerities—accompanied by other ascetics and sages like the Sanaka, as well as many devotees of Lord Vishnu such as Prahalād—approached Shrī Hanumān.

These great masters—who had attained to the pinnacle of their spiritual knowledge and were considered most wise and erudite—had come to Hanumān in order to get access to the highest knowledge; and they said unto Hanumān: "O thou mighty brave Lord; O son-of-the-wind-god, do please teach us: What is that ultimate essence which is known to those who are renowned experts in the knowledge pertaining to Brahmm? What is the basic tenet, the cardinal essence, the substantive edict of the eighteen Puranas, the eighteen sub-Puranas, and the Smritis? The four Vedas and all the scriptures are well known to thee—they have been taught to thee by none other than the sun-god. Thy knowledge is more comprehensive than that of anyone. Oh the valiant brave Hanumān, do please tell: What is the essence of all the great teachings? What is the fundamental knowledge expounded and enunciated by the scriptures?"

And Hanumān replied: "O ye exalted sages, seers, ascetics, and devotees of the Lord! Listen carefully to what I have to say. It has the potential of destroying sin, and rent asunder all fetters of this deluding fearsome Creation. It incorporates the essence of all that's at the heart of our scriptures and metaphysics. The very core of the tenets, axioms and maxims, the greatest principle amongst them, is the principle of Tārak-Brahmm—that form of Brahmm which delivers one from the torments associated with this seemingly endless cycles of births and deaths; which releases the soul from bondages and into complete bliss and felicity. Hear ye all and know: It is Rāma who is the supreme transcendental Brahmm. Rāma is that ultimate *'Tattwa'*—the essence, the fundamental aspect—which thou enquire of and seek. It is Shrī Rāma who is the Tārak Brahmm. Rāma is Brahmm personified, the embodiment of Supreme Consciousness & Bliss; Rāma is Para-Brahmm, the supreme austerity; Rāma is the Ultimate Essence of the Universe—the *Tārak-Brahmm*."

The sages enquired further and Hanumān detailed out to them the various aspects of the divine forms of Shrī Rāma. Those great sages, led by Sanaka, now wished to learn of the Mantras for meditating upon Rāma and said, "Oh thou strong, valiant son of Anjani! Lord Rāma is celebrated as Tārak—the Redeemer, and as Brahmm—the All-Pervading Supreme-Soul. We request thee to please teach to us his Divine Holy Mantras for our welfare—those Mantras through which one can meditate and worship the Tārak-Brahmm Rāma." And Hanumān graciously taught to them the various Mantras of Rāma.

The Four-Lettered Rāma Mantras are:

रामभद्र — rāma-bhadra

रामचंद्र — rāma-caṁdra

Like the Mantra राम (rāma), the *Rishī* (patron sage) of the Four-Lettered रामभद्र , रामचंद्र Rāma-Mantras is Brahammā—the Creator; the *chaṁda* (छँद—meter or poetic style) is—Gayatrī; and Rāma Himself is the *Devatā* (the patron deity) of these Mantras.

⌘⌘⌘⌘⌘

रामभद्र (rāma-bhadra), the Name of Lord Rama, is the first Four-Lettered Rāma Mantra. The Sanskrit word Bhadra means someone who is civilized. रामभद्र Rāmabhadra stands for Prince Rama, who is knightly, full of valor—and yet mannerly, regardful, reverent. रामभद्र stands for the unfearing King Rama, who is mighty & courageous—and yet humble, gracious, deferent. रामभद्र stands for Lord Rama, renowned to be most glorious, gallant, and fearsome in battle—and yet most benign, considerate, gentle.

Our Lord रामभद्र Rāmabhadra is adorned with innate nobility and grandeur—He is the Lord that is magnanimous and gentle; scholarly, learned, wise; noble and genteel—replete with all the auspicious virtues.

Righteous, pious, cultured—these describe the Majestic King Rama of Ayodhya, the embodied form of the Lord-God: the Honored-One—who at the same time gives honor; the Exalted-One—in whose very presence you yourself become exalted.

⌘⌘⌘⌘⌘

रामचंद्र (rāma-caṁdra), the name of Lord Rama, is the second of the Four-Lettered Rāma Mantras. The Sanskrit word Chandra stands for the moon; it is an epithet which signifies that special form of energy, splendor, brilliance which is simultaneously cool & tranquil.

During His advent, King Rama was called rāma-caṁdra रामचंद्र for He was beautiful, pleasing, spiritually assuasive. Everyone found Lord रामचंद्र to be charming and soothing—a Being as enchanting as the celestial Moon.

राम is the blazing element of Fire, splendorous as the Sun in power—and yet which showers down upon His devotees as रामचंद्र, the gentleness of Moon.

Verily रामचंद्र is alike the Moon—the celestial pitcher of Ambrosia; रामचंद्र is the elixir that imparts to us eternal life—full of never-ending bliss.

⌘ ⌘ ⌘ ⌘

Thus the Four-Lettered Mantras: रामभद्र, रामचंद्र —the Names of Rama—are used to meditate upon that aspect of the Lord-God which is benign, gentle, vestal.

Like Bhagwan Rama Himself, these रामभद्र, रामचंद्र Mantras of Rama are instinct with divinity and power of the Almighty—more so the healing, soothing, gracious, kind aspects which are full of ambrosial bliss.

From Brahmm—the Absolute-Supreme-Being, the Only-Existent-Consciousness—has issued forth everything that is found in Creation—from the glorious to the gory. That transcendental Causal Being—the ultimate reality, attributeless, and infinite, from whom everything has emerged—is most wonderful and of diverse hues.

राम is the personification of that Infinite Brahmm—but राम is the embodiment of that Brahmm in a human form and of human aspects, although replete with the powers of the Almighty God.

Even in the human advent, Rama still had diverse human hues which shone during His advent; and of that exalted born glorious Lord राम—who came as the personification of Dharma, the walking living breathing Vedas—रामभद्र & रामचंद्र represent the most benign, gracious, gentle human side of the Lord-God. He is the Lord who is gracious, genial, forgiving—although still instinct with all the powers manifest in the Almighty.

These Four-Lettered Rāma-Mantras रामभद्र , रामचंद्र are rife with tranquil power; they allow us to easily reach out to that energy which is otherwise extreme, glorious, and dynamic as fire—a radiant firestorm of the Sun that can be touched having become reflected through the Moon.

The Names रामभद्र & रामचंद्र are representative of kindness, gentleness, forgiveness, compassion, mercifulness, leniency, and suchlike gracious aspects of the Lord-God. The Japa of रामभद्र & रामचंद्र is therefore performed with a special view of finding deliverance from this turbulent world, for seeking forgiveness for our faults, for getting the pardon of God, for attaining to purity and gaining an everlasting peace of soul.

रामभद्र & रामचंद्र—these most soothing Mantras of Rama are the bestowers of happiness, blessing, bliss. The Japa of रामभद्र & रामचंद्र is performed with a view of receiving favor and grace of the Lord God, for the purpose of acquiring ease and gentleness in life, for attaining to tranquility.

Let us never forget: Rāma is Bliss and the Key to that Bliss is in the Name राम. The Rāma-Mantra राम is just like *Kalpa-Vriksha*, the wish-fulfilling Tree of Paradise; and whatever or whosoever becomes associated with राम gains enhancement in the shade of राम; and that's what we see with the words भद्र & चंद्र. In proximity of राम, the Sanskrit words भद्र & चंद्र themselves have become into powerful Mantras— रामभद्र & रामचंद्र —that have brought solace to humanity for Ages.

He who takes shelter of राम in complete faith obtains every blessing and gets what he seeks—such is the power of the राम Mantra. They who affectionately meditate upon राम go beyond sin; they go beyond sorrows; and they ever remain merged in that Bliss which is called राम.

obeisance to śrī-rāma

श्रीराघवं दशरथात्मजमप्रमेयं
śrī-rāghavaṁ daśarath-ātmajam-aprameyaṁ
सीतापतिं रघुकुलान्वयरत्नदीपम् ।
sītā-patiṁ raghu-kul-ānvaya-ratna-dīpam ,
आजानुबाहुमरविन्ददलायताक्षं
ājānu-bāhum-aravinda-dalāya-tākṣaṁ
रामं निशाचरविनाशकरं नमामि ॥
rāmaṁ niśācara-vināśa-karaṁ namāmi .

Bow I to Shrī-Rāma—son of Dasaratha, incomparable, the beloved consort of Sītā, the shining gem and leading light of the clan of Raghus—with long arms reaching upto His knees and eyes resembling petals of a lotus flower; unto Him Rāma, who is the annihilator of the night-wandering Rākshasas of the world, I offer salutations.

⌘

वैदेहीसहितं सुरद्रुमतले हैमे महामण्डपे
vaidehī-sahitaṁ sura-druma-tale haime mahā-maṇḍape
मध्ये पुष्पकमासने मणिमये वीरासने सुस्थितम् ।
madhye puṣpakam-āsane maṇi-maye vīr-āsane su-sthitam ,
अग्रे वाचयति प्रभञ्जनसुते तत्त्वं मुनिभ्यः परं
agre vāca-yati pra-bhañjana-sute tattvaṁ muni-bhyaḥ paraṁ
व्याख्यान्तं भरतादिभिः परिवृतं रामं भजे श्यामलम् ॥
vyākhy-āntaṁ bharat-ādibhiḥ pari-vṛtaṁ rāmaṁ bhaje śyāmalam .

I bow to Lord Rāma who—along with His beloved consort Sītā, daughter of Videha—is seated under the shade of Kalpavriksha (the Divine Wish-Tree) nestled in a grand gilded altar, set within the middle of the aerial Pushpaka Vimāna—upon a splendid throne constellated with gems. Encircled by brothers Bharatha and others, Rāma sits—well settled, sporting the posture of the bravest hero—while in front abides the son of Prabhanjana (Hanumān) standing in veneration, enunciating the grand maxim: that Rāma is the Supreme Truth sung of and extolled by sages.

⌘

श्रीरामो रामभद्रश्च रामचन्द्रश्च शाश्वतः ।
śrīrāmo **rāma-bhadra**-śca **rāma-candra**-śca śāśvataḥ ,
राजीवलोचनः श्रीमान् राजेन्द्रो रघुपुङ्गवः ॥ १ ॥
rājīva-locanaḥ śrīmān rājendro raghu-puṅgavaḥ .1.

Glory be to Shrī Rāma—Bestower of Felicity, Shrī Rāma-Bhadra—the all-auspicious Lord, Shrī Rāma-Candra—shining like the full-moon, the eternal Divine-Being of lotus-eyes, abode of Laxmi, King-of-Kings, the grand Scion of the Dynasty of Raghus.

[Above adapted from: Rama Hymns]

In case you are unfamiliar with Sanskrit, the following might prove useful.

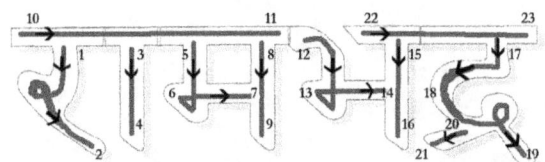

To write रामभद्र (rāma-bhadra) trace:

line 1-2 -- consonant र, which is the sound **r** in '**r**un'

line 3-4 -- long vowel आ (ā) in Matrā form, which is the sound **a** in '**a**rk'

line 5-6-7 & 8-9 -- consonant म, which is the sound **m** in '**m**ust'

line 10-11 -- this is the combined line (each consonant/vowel has a line at top)

[That completes राम —which in pronunciation rhymes with calm]

line 12-13-14 & 15-16 -- consonant भ, which is the sound **bh** in '**Bh**utan'

line 17-18-19 -- consonant द, which is the sound **th** in '**th**us'

line 20-21 -- consonant र in short form, which is the sound **r** in '**r**un'

line 22-23 -- the top line

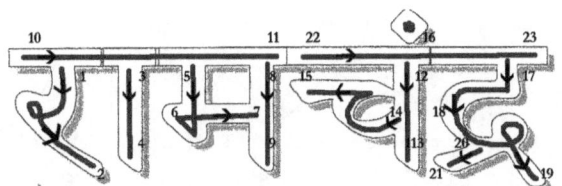

To write रामचंद्र (rāma-caṁdra) trace:

line 1-2 -- consonant र, which is the sound **r** in '**r**un'

line 3-4 -- long vowel आ (ā) in Matrā form, which is the sound **a** in '**a**rk'

line 5-6-7 & 8-9 -- consonant म, which is the sound **m** in '**m**ust'

line 10-11 -- this is the combined line (each consonant/vowel has a line at top)

[That completes राम —which in pronunciation rhymes with calm]

line 12-13 & 14-15 -- consonant च, which is the sound **ch** in '**ch**urch'

moon dot 16 -- chaṁdra bindu—the nasalized vowel ṁ which sounds like **n** in 'Lufthа**n**sa'

line 17-18-19 -- consonant द, which is the sound **th** in '**th**us'

line 20-21 -- consonant र in short form, which is the sound **r** in '**r**un'

line 22-23 -- the top line

रामभद्र रामभद्र रामभद्र रामभद्र रामभद्र रामभद्र रामभद्र

रामभद्र

रामभद्र रामभद्र रामभद्र रामभद्र रामभद्र रामभद्र रामभद्र

रामभद्र

रामचंद्र   रामचंद्र   रामचंद्र   रामचंद्र   रामचंद्र   रामचंद्र   रामचंद्र

रामचंद्र	रामचंद्र	रामचंद्र	रामचंद्र	रामचंद्र	रामचंद्र	रामचंद्र

रामचंद्र

Today's Date : _____

रामभद्र   रामभद्र   रामभद्र   रामभद्र   रामभद्र   रामभद्र   रामभद्र

रामभद्र

रामभद्र रामभद्र रामभद्र रामभद्र रामभद्र रामभद्र रामभद्र

रामभद्र

रामचंद्र रामचंद्र रामचंद्र रामचंद्र रामचंद्र रामचंद्र रामचंद्र

रामचंद्र

रामचंद्र रामचंद्र रामचंद्र रामचंद्र रामचंद्र रामचंद्र रामचंद्र

रामचंद्र

रामभद्र   रामभद्र   रामभद्र   रामभद्र   रामभद्र   रामभद्र   रामभद्र

रामभद्र

रामभद्र रामभद्र रामभद्र रामभद्र रामभद्र रामभद्र रामभद्र

रामचंद्र　　रामचंद्र　　रामचंद्र　　रामचंद्र　　रामचंद्र　　रामचंद्र　　रामचंद्र

रामचंद्र

रामचंद्र रामचंद्र रामचंद्र रामचंद्र रामचंद्र रामचंद्र रामचंद्र

रामचंद्र

रामभद्र   रामभद्र   रामभद्र   रामभद्र   रामभद्र   रामभद्र   रामभद्र

रामभद्र

रामभद्र रामभद्र रामभद्र रामभद्र रामभद्र रामभद्र रामभद्र

रामभद्र

रामचंद्र रामचंद्र रामचंद्र रामचंद्र रामचंद्र रामचंद्र रामचंद्र

रामचंद्र रामचंद्र रामचंद्र रामचंद्र रामचंद्र रामचंद्र रामचंद्र

रामचंद्र   रामचंद्र   रामचंद्र   रामचंद्र   रामचंद्र   रामचंद्र   रामचंद्र

रामचंद्र

| रामभद्र | रामभद्र | रामभद्र | रामभद्र | रामभद्र | रामभद्र | रामभद्र |

रामभद्र

रामभद्र रामभद्र रामभद्र रामभद्र रामभद्र रामभद्र रामभद्र

रामचंद्र　　रामचंद्र　　रामचंद्र　　रामचंद्र　　रामचंद्र　　रामचंद्र　　रामचंद्र

रामचंद्र

रामचंद्र　　रामचंद्र　　रामचंद्र　　रामचंद्र　　रामचंद्र　　रामचंद्र　　रामचंद्र

रामचंद्र　　रामचंद्र　　रामचंद्र　　रामचंद्र　　रामचंद्र　　रामचंद्र　　रामचंद्र

रामभद्र	रामभद्र	रामभद्र	रामभद्र	रामभद्र	रामभद्र	रामभद्र

रामभद्र

रामभद्र   रामभद्र   रामभद्र   रामभद्र   रामभद्र   रामभद्र   रामभद्र

रामभद्र

Today's Date : _____

रामचंद्र   रामचंद्र   रामचंद्र   रामचंद्र   रामचंद्र   रामचंद्र   रामचंद्र

रामचंद्र   रामचंद्र   रामचंद्र   रामचंद्र   रामचंद्र   रामचंद्र   रामचंद्र

रामचंद्र

रामभद्र   रामभद्र   रामभद्र   रामभद्र   रामभद्र   रामभद्र   रामभद्र

रामभद्र

रामभद्र   रामभद्र   रामभद्र   रामभद्र   रामभद्र   रामभद्र   रामभद्र

रामभद्र

रामचंद्र रामचंद्र रामचंद्र रामचंद्र रामचंद्र रामचंद्र रामचंद्र

रामचंद्र

रामचंद्र रामचंद्र रामचंद्र रामचंद्र रामचंद्र रामचंद्र

रामचंद्र   रामचंद्र   रामचंद्र   रामचंद्र   रामचंद्र   रामचंद्र   रामचंद्र

रामचंद्र

रामभद्र	रामभद्र	रामभद्र	रामभद्र	रामभद्र	रामभद्र	रामभद्र

रामभद्र

रामभद्र रामभद्र रामभद्र रामभद्र रामभद्र रामभद्र रामभद्र

रामचंद्र रामचंद्र रामचंद्र रामचंद्र रामचंद्र रामचंद्र रामचंद्र

रामचंद्र रामचंद्र रामचंद्र रामचंद्र रामचंद्र रामचंद्र रामचंद्र

रामचंद्र रामचंद्र रामचंद्र रामचंद्र रामचंद्र रामचंद्र रामचंद्र

रामचंद्र

रामभद्र रामभद्र रामभद्र रामभद्र रामभद्र रामभद्र रामभद्र

रामभद्र

रामभद्र रामभद्र रामभद्र रामभद्र रामभद्र रामभद्र रामभद्र

रामभद्र

Today's Date : _____

रामचंद्र   रामचंद्र   रामचंद्र   रामचंद्र   रामचंद्र   रामचंद्र   रामचंद्र

रामचंद्र रामचंद्र रामचंद्र रामचंद्र रामचंद्र रामचंद्र रामचंद्र

रामचंद्र

Today's Date : _____

रामभद्र रामभद्र रामभद्र रामभद्र रामभद्र रामभद्र रामभद्र

रामभद्र   रामभद्र   रामभद्र   रामभद्र   रामभद्र   रामभद्र   रामभद्र

रामभद्र

रामचंद्र   रामचंद्र   रामचंद्र   रामचंद्र   रामचंद्र   रामचंद्र   रामचंद्र

रामचंद्र

रामचंद्र रामचंद्र रामचंद्र रामचंद्र रामचंद्र रामचंद्र रामचंद्र

रामचंद्र

रामचंद्र रामचंद्र रामचंद्र रामचंद्र रामचंद्र रामचंद्र रामचंद्र

रामभद्र रामभद्र रामभद्र रामभद्र रामभद्र रामभद्र रामभद्र

रामभद्र रामभद्र रामभद्र रामभद्र रामभद्र रामभद्र रामभद्र

रामभद्र

रामचंद्र   रामचंद्र   रामचंद्र   रामचंद्र   रामचंद्र   रामचंद्र   रामचंद्र

रामचंद्र

रामचंद्र   रामचंद्र   रामचंद्र   रामचंद्र   रामचंद्र   रामचंद्र   रामचंद्र

रामचंद्र

रामभद्र　रामभद्र　रामभद्र　रामभद्र　रामभद्र　रामभद्र　रामभद्र

रामभद्र

रामभद्र रामभद्र रामभद्र रामभद्र रामभद्र रामभद्र रामभद्र

रामभद्र

रामचंद्र रामचंद्र रामचंद्र रामचंद्र रामचंद्र रामचंद्र रामचंद्र

रामचंद्र रामचंद्र रामचंद्र रामचंद्र रामचंद्र रामचंद्र रामचंद्र

रामचंद्र रामचंद्र रामचंद्र रामचंद्र रामचंद्र रामचंद्र रामचंद्र

रामचंद्र

रामभद्र रामभद्र रामभद्र रामभद्र रामभद्र रामभद्र रामभद्र

| रामभद्र | रामभद्र | रामभद्र | रामभद्र | रामभद्र | रामभद्र | रामभद्र |

रामभद्र

रामचंद्र रामचंद्र रामचंद्र रामचंद्र रामचंद्र रामचंद्र रामचंद्र

रामचंद्र रामचंद्र रामचंद्र रामचंद्र रामचंद्र रामचंद्र रामचंद्र

रामचंद्र

रामभद्र रामभद्र रामभद्र रामभद्र रामभद्र रामभद्र रामभद्र

रामभद्र

| रामभद्र | रामभद्र | रामभद्र | रामभद्र | रामभद्र | रामभद्र | रामभद्र |

रामभद्र

रामचंद्र रामचंद्र रामचंद्र रामचंद्र रामचंद्र रामचंद्र रामचंद्र

रामचंद्र रामचंद्र रामचंद्र रामचंद्र रामचंद्र रामचंद्र रामचंद्र

रामचंद्र   रामचंद्र   रामचंद्र   रामचंद्र   रामचंद्र   रामचंद्र   रामचंद्र

रामचंद्र

रामभद्र   रामभद्र   रामभद्र   रामभद्र   रामभद्र   रामभद्र   रामभद्र

रामभद्र

रामभद्र रामभद्र रामभद्र रामभद्र रामभद्र रामभद्र रामभद्र

रामभद्र

रामचंद्र	रामचंद्र	रामचंद्र	रामचंद्र	रामचंद्र	रामचंद्र	रामचंद्र

रामचंद्र

रामचंद्र   रामचंद्र   रामचंद्र   रामचंद्र   रामचंद्र   रामचंद्र   रामचंद्र

रामचंद्र

Today's Date : _____

| रामभद्र | रामभद्र | रामभद्र | रामभद्र | रामभद्र | रामभद्र | रामभद्र |

रामभद्र

रामभद्र	रामभद्र	रामभद्र	रामभद्र	रामभद्र	रामभद्र	रामभद्र

रामभद्र

रामचंद्र   रामचंद्र   रामचंद्र   रामचंद्र   रामचंद्र   रामचंद्र   रामचंद्र

रामचंद्र

रामचंद्र   रामचंद्र   रामचंद्र   रामचंद्र   रामचंद्र   रामचंद्र   रामचंद्र

रामचंद्र

रामभद्र　रामभद्र　रामभद्र　रामभद्र　रामभद्र　रामभद्र　रामभद्र

रामभद्र

रामभद्र रामभद्र रामभद्र रामभद्र रामभद्र रामभद्र रामभद्र

रामभद्र

रामचंद्र   रामचंद्र   रामचंद्र   रामचंद्र   रामचंद्र   रामचंद्र   रामचंद्र

रामचंद्र

रामचंद्र   रामचंद्र   रामचंद्र   रामचंद्र   रामचंद्र   रामचंद्र   रामचंद्र

रामचंद्र

रामभद्र   रामभद्र   रामभद्र   रामभद्र   रामभद्र   रामभद्र   रामभद्र

रामभद्र

रामभद्र रामभद्र रामभद्र रामभद्र रामभद्र रामभद्र रामभद्र

रामभद्र

रामचंद्र   रामचंद्र   रामचंद्र   रामचंद्र   रामचंद्र   रामचंद्र   रामचंद्र

रामचंद्र

रामचंद्र   रामचंद्र   रामचंद्र   रामचंद्र   रामचंद्र   रामचंद्र   रामचंद्र

रामचंद्र

Today's Date : _____

रामभद्र	रामभद्र	रामभद्र	रामभद्र	रामभद्र	रामभद्र	रामभद्र

रामभद्र

रामभद्र रामभद्र रामभद्र रामभद्र रामभद्र रामभद्र रामभद्र

रामभद्र

Today's Date : _____

रामचंद्र   रामचंद्र   रामचंद्र   रामचंद्र   रामचंद्र   रामचंद्र   रामचंद्र

रामचंद्र   रामचंद्र   रामचंद्र   रामचंद्र   रामचंद्र   रामचंद्र   रामचंद्र

रामचंद्र रामचंद्र रामचंद्र रामचंद्र रामचंद्र रामचंद्र रामचंद्र

रामचंद्र

Today's Date : _____

रामभद्र　रामभद्र　रामभद्र　रामभद्र　रामभद्र　रामभद्र　रामभद्र

रामभद्र

रामभद्र रामभद्र रामभद्र रामभद्र रामभद्र रामभद्र रामभद्र

रामभद्र

Today's Date : _____

रामचंद्र रामचंद्र रामचंद्र रामचंद्र रामचंद्र रामचंद्र रामचंद्र

रामचंद्र

रामचंद्र   रामचंद्र   रामचंद्र   रामचंद्र   रामचंद्र   रामचंद्र   रामचंद्र

रामचंद्र

रामभद्र रामभद्र रामभद्र रामभद्र रामभद्र रामभद्र रामभद्र

रामभद्र रामभद्र रामभद्र रामभद्र रामभद्र रामभद्र रामभद्र

रामभद्र

रामचंद्र रामचंद्र रामचंद्र रामचंद्र रामचंद्र रामचंद्र रामचंद्र

रामचंद्र

रामचंद्र रामचंद्र रामचंद्र रामचंद्र रामचंद्र रामचंद्र रामचंद्र

रामचंद्र रामचंद्र रामचंद्र रामचंद्र रामचंद्र रामचंद्र रामचंद्र

रामचंद्र

Today's Date : _____

रामभद्र रामभद्र रामभद्र रामभद्र रामभद्र रामभद्र रामभद्र

रामभद्र रामभद्र रामभद्र रामभद्र रामभद्र रामभद्र रामभद्र

रामभद्र

रामचंद्र रामचंद्र रामचंद्र रामचंद्र रामचंद्र रामचंद्र रामचंद्र

रामचंद्र

रामचंद्र　रामचंद्र　रामचंद्र　रामचंद्र　रामचंद्र　रामचंद्र　रामचंद्र

रामचंद्र

| रामभद्र | रामभद्र | रामभद्र | रामभद्र | रामभद्र | रामभद्र | रामभद्र |

रामभद्र

रामभद्र   रामभद्र   रामभद्र   रामभद्र   रामभद्र   रामभद्र   रामभद्र

रामभद्र

रामचंद्र   रामचंद्र   रामचंद्र   रामचंद्र   रामचंद्र   रामचंद्र   रामचंद्र

रामचंद्र

रामचंद्र   रामचंद्र   रामचंद्र   रामचंद्र   रामचंद्र   रामचंद्र   रामचंद्र

रामचंद्र रामचंद्र रामचंद्र रामचंद्र रामचंद्र रामचंद्र रामचंद्र

रामचंद्र

Today's Date : _____

रामभद्र   रामभद्र   रामभद्र   रामभद्र   रामभद्र   रामभद्र   रामभद्र

रामभद्र

रामभद्र रामभद्र रामभद्र रामभद्र रामभद्र रामभद्र रामभद्र

रामभद्र

रामचंद्र रामचंद्र रामचंद्र रामचंद्र रामचंद्र रामचंद्र रामचंद्र

रामचंद्र

रामचंद्र	रामचंद्र	रामचंद्र	रामचंद्र	रामचंद्र	रामचंद्र	रामचंद्र

रामचंद्र

रामभद्र   रामभद्र   रामभद्र   रामभद्र   रामभद्र   रामभद्र   रामभद्र

रामभद्र

www.ingramcontent.com/pod-product-compliance
Lightning Source LLC
Chambersburg PA
CBHW051754100526
44591CB00017B/2695